The fantastically feminist
(and totally true) story of the
ASTOUNDING ACTOR
AND ACTIVIST

EMMA WATSON

ANNA DohERty

wren
& rook

MEET EMMA'S
Family and Friends

Jacqueline Luesby
1959 – now

Jacqueline is always very supportive of all Emma does, both in her acting and activism. One time they even fly all the way from England to Washington, US, just to take part in a Women's March together!

Emma
1990 – now

Dan is the main character in the Harry Potter films alongside Emma. He gets the part after the producer meets him in a theatre.

Rupert also stars in Harry Potter with Emma. For his very first audition for the film he sends a video of himself rapping!

Daniel Radcliffe
1989 – now

Rupert Grint
1988 – now

Chris is an excellent book narrator - he does all the voices when he reads to Emma when she's little.

Chris Watson
1959 – now

Alex
1992 – now

Emma and Alex are very close! He accompanies her to a few film premieres and even plays an extra (a background character) in Harry Potter!

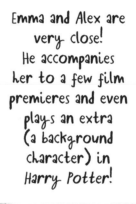

Twins! They both play the younger version of Emma's character in the film Ballet Shoes (2007).

Toby
2003 – now

Lucy
2004 – now

Nina
2004 – now

1990

Emma Charlotte Duerre Watson is born
in Paris, in France. She has a mum and
a dad who are both super-clever lawyers,
and soon she also has a little brother
called Alex.

OXFORD

OFF TO LONDON

DAd's New FLAT

1995

When her parents decide to separate, the whole family moves to England. Emma, Alex and her mum live in Oxford. But her dad lives in London, so Emma and Alex spend a lot of time zooming across the country to visit him. They read to pass the time – Emma particularly loves the *Harry Potter* books, about a boy wizard and his adventures at his magical school.

HOCKEY

DANCE CLASS

1995

Emma starts school and throws herself into every activity she can – running around on the hockey field, tip-tapping through dance classes, performing in plays, winning poetry prizes – as well as working hard to get the best grades!

PERFORMING

POETRY

1999

One day at school, auditions are announced for the new *Harry Potter* film.

Girls who want to be considered line up in the school gym and have their photo taken.

Emma is desperate and determined to play Hermione, one of Harry's best friends in the books. She is a fabulous character: she's enormously clever, works incredibly hard at school, and is extremely dedicated to all she puts her mind to … just like Emma!

Bright, eager, hard-working Emma thinks they are so similar in personality that she HAS to get the part! She practises scenes for hours and hours each day until she is absolutely perfect.

EMMA
(HERMiONe)

RUPERT
(RON)

DAN
(HARRY)

After eight long, nerve-wracking auditions, Emma wins the role! She is head-over-heels thrilled. She is cast alongside two boys: Daniel Radcliffe as Harry and Rupert Grint as Ron (Harry's other best friend).

2000

Filming starts! Emma has to have her hair dyed darker and styled to look bushy so she looks more like her character.

As always, Emma tries her absolute best – in fact she works so hard that she even learns Dan and Rupert's lines too! Sometimes the director has to ask them to film a scene again because Emma is mouthing along to the boys!

The trio hang out in between takes, playing cheeky pranks on each other and competing in table tennis matches.

Emma thinks the boys are like extra brothers. She sneakily watches movies all night with Dan, and guzzles chocolate with Rupert.

It's not all fun and glamorous shooting so many films – eight in ten years! The children are away from home and miss a lot of school. They have lessons on set, sometimes for up to five hours a day.

It's a jam-packed time for Emma: one minute she will be waving a wand, the next memorising maths. Can you imagine!

Emma is delighted that she can learn in between filming scenes because although she loves acting, she equally adores school. She is determined to get the best grades she can so she can apply to a brilliant university.

7 x 1 = 7
7 x 2 = 14
7 x 3 = 21
7 x 4 = 28
7 x 5 = 35
7 x 6 = 42
7 x 7 = 49
7 x 8 = 56
7 x 9 = 63
7 x 10 = 70

WANDS AWAY PLEASE

PUT THEM BACK IN THE PROP DEPARTMENT

MATHS WORK
6 x 2 = 12
9 x 2 = 18
4 x 2 = 8
HOMEWORK EMMA

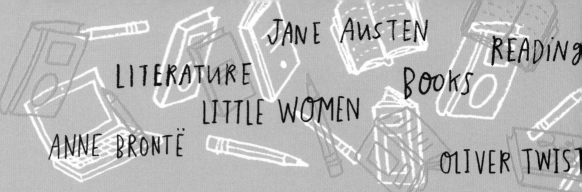

LITERATURE
JANE AUSTEN
LITTLE WOMEN
READING
BOOKS
ANNE BRONTË
OLIVER TWIST

2009

Bookworm Emma starts studying English Literature at Brown University in the US, which means she gets to read lots and lots. She keeps juggling working as an actor and learning, because she believes education is incredibly important. Sometimes she'll be on TV late one evening and in class early the next morning!

Although she's cramming as much acting and studying into her days as she can, she still leaves time to have fun, performing in student plays and throwing parties for her friends. What a busy bee!

In some places around the globe, it's not common for girls to go to school, but Emma passionately believes that girls and boys should have an equal chance to be educated.

Often boys are given better opportunities, better education and better-paid jobs, just because they are boys. That's not fair! Girls miss out on these chances for many reasons: they may have to stay at home to do housework, they may not be expected to have a job when they grow up and have their own family, or in some places even travelling to school may be too dangerous.

If girls can go to school, they can get a job, earn their own money and do whatever they want when they grow up. Just going to school is a step towards a more equal world.

LET GIRLS go to SCHOOL

Determined to make a change, Emma visits Zambia with a charity that works in rural parts of Africa teaching people about how important it is that girls get to learn.

2014

Emma is made UN Women Goodwill Ambassador. Her job is to work for gender equality (this means making everything equally fair for everyone, whether they are man or woman, boy or girl) and the empowerment of women (helping girls and women to stand up for themselves and to enjoy the same rights as men).

One of the first things Emma does in this job is make a speech for the campaign HeForShe. HeForShe encourages everyone to fight for a fairer world, and especially encourages men and boys to join in.

After her brilliant speech, some people on the internet and in the news are really mean, but this only makes her more determined to work hard. These are the kind of attitudes she wants to change!

2015

Cast as Belle in *Beauty and the Beast*, Emma enthusiastically works to make Belle a positive character that girls can look up to.

Belle is a kind, determined, daydreaming, unconventional bookworm, but Emma thinks she can have even more girl power!

She thinks Belle should have a job, so convinces the film director to add in the backstory that Belle is an inventor. She encourages the costume designers to make Belle's clothes practical, for example wearing shoes that she can run in, having pockets in her dress and wearing bloomers so Belle doesn't have to worry about pulling up her skirt as she scampers around the film set. She wants Belle to be a fantastically feminist role model!

NATURAL DYE

A—

EASIER TO RUN IN

Emma also persuades the designers to make the costumes in ways that are as environmentally friendly as possible. They even colour some of them with vegetable dye!

The film premieres in cinemas in 2017 and is a huge success!

2016

Mixing together two of her passions, Emma starts Our Shared Shelf – a feminist book group!

It's an online space for people to share thoughts about feminism – ideas about what changes need to be made so that men, women and everyone are treated equally and have equal chances in life. People from all over the world can talk about anything, such as feminism in different countries, why they are angry that things aren't equal – or just whether they liked the book or not!

Sometimes people don't get involved in talking about feminism because they don't have anyone to talk about it with, or they don't feel like they know enough, or they don't think it is their problem to fix. The great thing about Our Shared Shelf is anyone can join, so it's a fun, unique and easy way to get more people involved in talking about feminism.

TIME'S UP

2018

Emma becomes a very active member of Time's Up.

Time's Up is about making work a safe and fair place for women, and it supports women who have been treated very badly in the past just because they are female. It does all sorts of things, like teaching people about treating each other better and respecting everyone the same, raising awareness, and helping women who have been treated badly at work.

They've only been going for a short time, but they have achieved lots already!

Emma

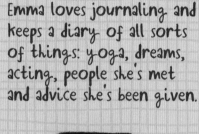

She's even a fashion designer, creating a Fairtrade collection for People Tree that launched in 2010.

Emma loves journaling and keeps a diary of all sorts of things: yoga, dreams, acting, people she's met and advice she's been given.

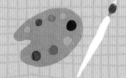

She loves painting.

Her absolute favourite *Harry Potter* book is *The Prisoner of Azkaban*.

Emma missed the after-party for the Oscars in 2014 because she accidentally fell asleep nibbling on pizza in her hotel room!

Emma loves animals. She used to visit the creatures on the *Harry Potter* set between takes and even had her own cats, Bubbles and Domino, back home.

Since 2015, she has tried to wear only sustainable fashion on the red carpet!

Amazing Emma has won a whole bunch of awards, including the first acting award that includes everyone, and doesn't divide winners into male and female, in 2017!

Apart from Harry Potter and Beauty and the Beast, Emma has acted in lots of other films, such as Little Women (2019).

When she was growing up, Emma adored Roald Dahl's books.

Not only is she super fashionable, Emma has also been a model.

The Fantastically FEMiNist Emma Watson

Emma is fantastically feminist because she gives 100 per cent to causes she believes in. She is determined to achieve equality and dedicates so much of her time to making the world a better place for everyone, especially girls and women.

Emma knows she's got a fabulous and lucky life as an actor, and she uses her fame as a way to spread her message. As well as travelling around the world educating and talking to people about her ideas, Emma tries to make her film characters be the best role models they can be for girls and women – from making practical adaptations to characters (for example, Emma insists on Belle having sensible dresses and shoes so she can do all sorts of fun things without having to worry about her clothes) to choosing to play characters who have a positive girl-power personality. Belle is curious, kind, creative and open-minded. Hermione is stubborn, determined, loyal and academic. And these are all qualities Emma has too!

Another trait she shares with Hermione is that Emma devours books. She especially likes books she can learn from, particularly about gender and feminism. She even took time off acting to read more, studying gender and feminism, teaching herself as much as she could. Through Our Shared Shelf, she spends time talking to people she can learn from. She's brilliant because she'll not rest until she knows as much about the subject as she can, so she can have the best chance of educating others about it.

She is always trying to find new and unusual ways to make people talk to each other about feminism, and she involves anyone and everyone. Her book club is free and open to all, because Emma believes everyone should have equal opportunities.

Emma wants to help spread her dream of gender equality because growing up she was aware that people treated her differently because she is a girl. She was called 'bossy' whereas boys were not. Teenage girls around her gave up sports so they didn't look muscly, and teenage boys stopped talking about their feelings. And when she was older, she noticed that the media talked a lot about her looks rather than all the great things she was doing.

Emma knows that a lot of people don't really understand 'feminism'. Really it is just campaigning for men and women to be treated equally. And Emma wants equal opportunities and equal chances for men and women in **everything**: from schooling, to talking about feelings, to how much they get paid, to what words are used to describe them.

Emma draws attention to her favourite causes in unusual and surprising ways. For example, she appeared at an award ceremony with black feminist activist Marai Larasi as her guest, and she gave advice to strangers through an iPad in a busy New York train station in exchange for a donation to charity.

Emma's enthusiasm, passion and friendliness make people want to listen and want to take part in her campaigns. Her creativity, open-mindedness, determination and eagerness to keep learning and educating others are what make her so brilliant and amazing. Her approach to feminism is fresh and inspiring. Who knows what fantastically feminist Emma will dream up and achieve next?

For Greta and Ariella

First published in Great Britain in 2020 by Wren & Rook

HB ISBN: 978 1 5263 6112 7
PB ISBN: 978 1 5263 6113 4
E-book ISBN: 978 1 5263 6114 1
1 3 5 7 9 10 8 6 4 2

MIX
Paper from
responsible sources
FSC® C104740

Wren & Rook
An imprint of
Hachette Children's Group
Part of Hodder & Stoughton
Carmelite House
50 Victoria Embankment
London EC4Y 0DZ

An Hachette UK Company
www.hachette.co.uk
www.hachettechildrens.co.uk

Printed in China